THE ULTIMATE BEGINNER

AIR FRYER COOKING

Easy, Low-Calorie, Dump-and-Go Recipes with Vibrant Full-Color
Images and 30-Day Meal Plan – Fry, Roast, and Bake Using
Pantry Staples for Couples, Families, and Everyday Meals

Sophia Holm

The Ultimate Beginner's Guide to

AIR FRYER
Cooking

FULLY COLORED PICTURES

Sophia Holm

Copyright Disclaimer

The Ultimate Beginner's Guide to Air Fryer Cooking: Easy, Low-Calorie, Dump-and-Go Recipes with Vibrant Full-Color Images and a 30-Day Meal Plan – Fry, Roast, and Bake Using Pantry Staples for Couples, Families, and Everyday Meals

For permissions, requests, or inquiries, please contact:
kdpmasterinc@gmail.com
First Edition: 2024

Published by [KDP MASTER INC]

CONTENTS

A Journey to Effortless, Delicious Air Fryer Cooking

Welcome to **The Ultimate Beginner's Guide to Air Fryer Cooking**, where healthy meets easy, and everyday meals become extraordinary. Imagine coming home after a long day, craving something comforting yet nutritious, and having the power to make it in minutes—crispy, flavorful, and perfectly cooked—all without breaking a sweat. This is what your air fryer can do for you, and this book is here to show you how.

Cooking doesn't have to be a chore. With the right tools and recipes, it can become a joyful experience, something you look forward to each day. Whether you're preparing a quick breakfast, a hearty lunch, or a delectable dinner, this guide is designed to make the process as simple as possible. From vibrant full-color images that inspire your creativity to easy-to-follow dump-and-go recipes that fit seamlessly into your busy life, everything in this book is crafted to help you make the most of your air fryer.

The air fryer has revolutionized the way we cook, giving us the ability to fry, roast, and bake with just a fraction of the oil used in traditional methods—all while keeping our meals delicious and nutritious. Whether you're a couple cooking together, a busy family trying to keep up with hectic schedules, or an individual just starting your cooking journey, this book is filled with low-calorie recipes that cater to everyone.

Inside, you'll find a diverse array of recipes featuring ingredients you already have in your pantry. No need for exotic or hard-to-find components—just simple, budget-friendly ingredients that are transformed into dishes bursting with flavor. With a 30-Day Meal Plan, we've taken the guesswork out of meal preparation, offering you a stress-free guide to creating balanced, nutritious meals every day.

Our goal is to empower you to use your air fryer confidently, to explore new flavors, and to enjoy every step of the cooking process. With each recipe accompanied by a vibrant photo, you can see just how tempting healthy eating can be. The multiple cooking techniques covered—frying, roasting, and baking—will help you unlock the true potential of your air fryer, making it your go-to kitchen companion.

Whether you're a complete novice or someone looking to expand their culinary skills, this book will inspire you to make cooking both healthy and fun. Let's embark on this journey together, one easy, flavorful meal at a time. Get ready to discover just how simple it is to bring wholesome, colorful, and mouthwatering dishes to your table—day after day.

So grab your air fryer, stock your pantry, and let's start cooking! Your journey to stress-free, flavorful, and healthy meals begins now.

CHAPTER 1
Air Fryer Basics

Introduction to Air Fryers

The air fryer is one of the most revolutionary kitchen appliances of the last decade. It has transformed the way we cook by providing a healthy, fast, and convenient alternative to traditional frying. Whether you're an experienced home cook or a complete beginner, understanding the basics of your air fryer will help you make the most of this powerful tool. This chapter will cover different types of air fryers, how they work, how to set them up, various cooking methods, and their advantages and disadvantages.

Types of Air Fryers

Air fryers come in several styles, each designed to suit different needs, cooking capacities, and preferences. Understanding the different types can help you choose the one that fits your cooking habits best.

 Basket Air Fryers:

- **Description:** The basket air fryer is the most popular type. It features a removable basket where food is placed, allowing for hot air to circulate evenly around the food.
- **Best For:** Crispy foods like fries, chicken wings, or roasted vegetables.
- **Pros:** Compact, easy to use, and provides evenly crisp results.
- **Cons:** Limited cooking capacity, best for smaller portions.

 Toaster Oven Air Fryers:

- **Description:** These air fryers resemble a small convection oven and often include multiple cooking functions such as baking, toasting, broiling, and even dehydrating.
- **Best For:** Larger batches, baking, and cooking multiple items at once.
- **Pros:** Versatile, spacious, great for multi-purpose use.
- **Cons:** Takes up more counter space and may have a learning curve due to its versatility.

Paddle Air Fryers:

- **Description:** These air fryers feature an internal paddle that automatically stirs food while it cooks, ensuring even crisping.
- **Best For:** Foods that need frequent stirring, such as risotto or fried rice.
- **Pros:** Hands-free cooking, eliminates the need to shake or stir manually.
- **Cons:** Limited in the types of foods it can accommodate, especially delicate items.

 Air Fryer Pressure Cookers:

- **Description:** Combining the functionality of a pressure cooker with an air fryer lid, these units are designed to save time while offering a variety of cooking options.
- **Best For:** One-pot meals, soups, and dishes that require both pressure cooking and crisping.
- **Pros:** Extremely versatile, allows you to prepare meals quickly.
- **Cons:** Larger in size, and can be more expensive than traditional air fryers.

How Does an Air Fryer Work?

An air fryer functions similarly to a convection oven, using a heating element and a high-powered fan to circulate hot air rapidly around the food. This rapid circulation, combined with the small amount of oil used, creates a crispy, golden exterior similar to deep-fried foods without the excessive use of oil.

Step-by-Step Process:
1. **Heating Element:** The air fryer's heating element, located at the top of the appliance, generates intense heat.

2. **Fan Circulation:** The fan above the heating element blows the hot air downwards and around the food.

3. **Maillard Reaction:** This rapid circulation and high heat cause the exterior of the food to brown and caramelize, producing that familiar crispy texture.

Setting Up Your Air Fryer

Setting up your air fryer is simple, but taking the time to do it properly can help ensure you get the best results.

1. **Unboxing and Placement:**
   - Remove all packaging, stickers, and labels from the air fryer.
   - Place the air fryer on a flat, heat-resistant surface with enough space around it to allow proper ventilation.

2. **Initial Cleaning:**
   - Wash the basket, tray, and any removable accessories in warm, soapy water, and allow them to dry completely.
   - Wipe down the interior and exterior with a damp cloth.

3. **Trial Run:**
   - Before cooking, run the air fryer empty at 350°F (175°C) for 5-10 minutes to remove any residual manufacturing odors.
   - This step will help ensure that your food doesn't pick up any unwanted smells or flavors.

Cooking Methods with an Air Fryer

An air fryer can handle a variety of cooking techniques, making it an incredibly versatile tool for daily use.

1. **Frying:**
   - Create crispy foods like French fries, chicken wings, and onion rings with minimal oil. The rapid air circulation allows for even crisping without the need for deep frying.

2. **Roasting:**
   - Roasting vegetables, such as Brussels sprouts, carrots, and sweet potatoes, is easy with the air fryer. The high heat and quick cooking time caramelize vegetables for rich flavor.

3. **Baking:**
   - Small baked goods, such as muffins, cookies, and even bread, can be baked in an air fryer. The compact space of the air fryer allows baked goods to rise quickly and cook evenly.

4. **Grilling:**
   - The air fryer can also grill foods like chicken breasts, fish, and steaks, giving them a delicious charred exterior without the need for a traditional grill.

5. **Reheating:**
   - Reheating leftovers in the air fryer restores their original crispiness, making it far superior to using a microwave, which often leaves food soggy.

Advantages of Using an Air Fryer

1. **Healthier Cooking:**
   - Air frying allows you to cook with up to 80% less oil compared to traditional frying, reducing fat and calories while still providing the taste and texture of fried food.

2. **Versatility:**
   - With the ability to fry, bake, roast, and grill, the air fryer is perfect for a wide range of recipes—from breakfast to dessert.

3. **Speed:**
   - The rapid air circulation allows for faster cooking times compared to conventional ovens, saving you valuable time in the kitchen.

4. **Ease of Use:**
   - The simple interface, often with preset options, makes air fryers user-friendly for all levels of cooking experience.

5. **Easy Cleanup:**
   - Most air fryer baskets and trays are non-stick and dishwasher-safe, making cleaning up after cooking a breeze.

Disadvantages of Using an Air Fryer

1. **Limited Capacity:**
   - Many basket-style air fryers have limited cooking space, which can be challenging when cooking for a large family or for batch cooking.

2. **Requires Some Trial and Error:**
   - Cooking times and temperatures may vary between air fryer models, and it may take some experimentation to get your recipes just right.

3. **Counter Space:**
   - Air fryers can take up significant counter space, which may be a concern for those with small kitchens.

4. **Texture Limitations:**
   - While air fryers do an excellent job of mimicking fried textures, certain dishes may lack the richness and depth of flavor that traditional deep frying provides.

Tips for Air Fryer Success

① Do Not Overcrowd the Basket: To achieve the best results, cook food in a single layer to ensure even cooking and crispiness.

② Use Oil Wisely: A light spray of oil is enough to enhance crispiness without adding excess calories. However, avoid using aerosol sprays that can damage the non-stick coating.

③ Preheat the Air Fryer: Preheating ensures even cooking and gives foods a better texture, especially when roasting vegetables or baking.

④ Shake or Flip Halfway Through Cooking: Shaking the basket or flipping the food halfway through helps to achieve consistent results.

Conclusion

Your air fryer is a versatile kitchen companion, capable of much more than just frying. With a few simple techniques, you can use it to make delicious, healthy meals with minimal effort. Whether you're roasting vegetables, baking muffins, or grilling chicken, the air fryer will save you time while enhancing the flavor of your food. Now that you understand the basics, it's time to put your air fryer to work—explore the upcoming chapters and discover a world of flavorful, easy-to-make recipes that will turn everyday cooking into an enjoyable experience.

Chapter 2: Breakfast Favourites

Sweet Potato Breakfast Hash

 Yield: 4 servings   *Prep Time:* 5 minutes   *Cook Time:* 15 minutes   *Temperature:* 400°F (200°C) *Cooking method:* Roast

INGREDIENTS

- 2 medium sweet potatoes, diced (about 1-inch pieces)
- 1/2 tsp smoked paprika
- 1/2 tsp garlic powder
- Salt and pepper, to taste
- 1 tbsp olive oil

DIRECTIONS

1. Preheat the air fryer to 400°F (200°C).
2. Toss the diced sweet potatoes with olive oil, smoked paprika, garlic powder, salt, and pepper.
3. Place the sweet potatoes in the air fryer basket and roast for 15 minutes, shaking halfway through.
4. Serve warm.

Nutritional Information

120 calories, 2g protein, 20g carbohydrates, 4g fat, 3g fiber, 0mg cholesterol, 200mg sodium, 450mg potassium.

Egg and Spinach Breakfast Cups

Yield: 4 servings

Prep Time: 5 minutes

Cook Time: 10 minutes

Temperature: 350°F (175°C)

Cooking method: Bake

INGREDIENTS

- 4 large eggs
- 1 cup fresh spinach, chopped
- 1/4 cup grated Parmesan cheese
- Salt and pepper, to taste

DIRECTIONS

1. Preheat the air fryer to 350°F (175°C).
2. In a bowl, whisk together the eggs, spinach, Parmesan, salt, and pepper.
3. Pour the mixture into silicone muffin cups.
4. Place the muffin cups in the air fryer basket and cook for 10 minutes or until set.
5. Let cool slightly before serving.

Nutritional Information

90 calories, 7g protein, 2g carbohydrates, 6g fat, 1g fiber, 180mg cholesterol, 150mg sodium, 100mg potassium

Greek Yogurt Pancakes

Yield:
3 servings

Prep Time:
5 minutes

Cook Time:
10 minutes

Temperature:
360°F (180°C)

Cooking method:
Fry

INGREDIENTS

- 1 cup Greek yogurt
- 1/2 cup all-purpose flour
- 1 large egg
- 1/2 tsp baking powder

DIRECTIONS

1. Preheat the air fryer to 360°F (180°C).
2. Mix together Greek yogurt, flour, egg, and baking powder until smooth.
3. Form small pancakes and place them on parchment paper in the air fryer basket.
4. Cook for 5 minutes per side or until golden brown.
5. Serve with fresh berries or honey.

Nutritional Information

120 calories, 7g protein, 16g carbohydrates, 4g fat, 1g fiber,
50mg cholesterol, 70mg sodium, 60mg potassium.

Berry-Stuffed French Toast

 Yield: 4 servings   **Prep Time:** 5 minutes   **Cook Time:** 8 minutes   **Temperature:** 360°F (180°C)   **Cooking method:** Bake

INGREDIENTS

- 4 slices whole wheat bread
- 1/2 cup mixed berries (blueberries, strawberries)
- 2 large eggs
- 1/4 cup unsweetened almond milk
- 1/2 tsp vanilla extract

DIRECTIONS

1. Preheat the air fryer to 360°F (180°C).
2. Spread berries evenly between 2 slices of bread, then top with the remaining slices to make sandwiches.
3. Whisk together the eggs, almond milk, and vanilla in a shallow dish. Dip each sandwich in the egg mixture.
4. Place sandwiches in the air fryer basket and bake for 8 minutes, flipping halfway through.
5. Serve warm.

Nutritional Information

160 calories, 7g protein, 20g carbohydrates, 5g fat, 3g fiber, 90mg cholesterol, 160mg sodium, 150mg potassium.

Breakfast Sausage Patties

 Yield:
4 servings

 Prep Time:
5 minutes

 Cook Time:
10 minutes

 Temperature:
375°F (190°C)

 **Cooking method:**
Fry

INGREDIENTS

- 1 lb ground turkey
- 1/2 tsp dried sage
- 1/2 tsp garlic powder
- 1/4 tsp black pepper
- Salt, to taste

DIRECTIONS

1. Preheat the air fryer to 375°F (190°C).
2. In a bowl, mix together the ground turkey, sage, garlic powder, black pepper, and salt.
3. Form the mixture into 8 small patties.
4. Place the patties in the air fryer basket and fry for 10 minutes, flipping halfway through.
5. Serve hot.

Nutritional Information

130 calories, 18g protein, 1g carbohydrates, 7g fat, 0g fiber,
60mg cholesterol, 150mg sodium, 250mg potassium.

Breakfast Burritos

 Yield:
4 servings

 Prep Time:
5 minutes

 Cook Time:
10 minutes

Temperature:
375°F (190°C)

 Cooking method:
Bake

INGREDIENTS

- 4 whole wheat tortillas
- 4 large eggs
- 1/2 cup diced bell pepper
- 1/2 cup shredded cheddar cheese
- 1/4 cup salsa

DIRECTIONS

1. Preheat the air fryer to 375°F (190°C).
2. In a bowl, whisk the eggs, then scramble in a skillet over medium heat until fully cooked.
3. Place scrambled eggs, diced bell pepper, cheddar cheese, and salsa in the center of each tortilla. Roll tightly into burritos.
4. Place burritos in the air fryer basket and bake for 5-7 minutes until crispy.
5. Serve warm.

Nutritional Information

220 calories, 12g protein, 22g carbohydrates, 10g fat, 2g fiber,
180mg cholesterol, 250mg sodium, 200mg potassium.

Avocado Toast with Eggs

Yield: 2 servings

Prep Time: 5 minutes

Cook Time: 6 minutes

Temperature: 350°F (175°C)

Cooking method: Bake

INGREDIENTS

- 2 slices whole grain bread
- 1 ripe avocado
- 2 large eggs
- Salt and pepper, to taste
- Red pepper flakes (optional)

DIRECTIONS

1. Preheat the air fryer to 350°F (175°C).
2. Toast the bread slices in the air fryer for 2 minutes.
3. In the meantime, mash the avocado with salt and pepper.
4. Spread the avocado on toasted bread, crack an egg on top of each slice, and place in the air fryer for 4 minutes or until eggs are set.
5. Sprinkle with red pepper flakes if desired and serve.

Nutritional Information

200 calories, 8g protein, 18g carbohydrates, 12g fat, 5g fiber, 190mg cholesterol, 150mg sodium, 350mg potassium.

Cinnamon Apple Rings

Yield: 4 servings | **Prep Time:** 5 minutes | **Cook Time:** 8 minutes | **Temperature:** 370°F (185°C) | **Cooking method:** Bake

INGREDIENTS

- 2 large apples, cored and sliced into rings
- 1/2 tsp ground cinnamon
- 1 tbsp melted coconut oil

DIRECTIONS

1. Preheat the air fryer to 370°F (185°C).
2. In a bowl, toss the apple rings with melted coconut oil and cinnamon.
3. Place the apple rings in the air fryer basket in a single layer and bake for 8 minutes, flipping halfway through.
4. Serve warm.

Nutritional Information

80 calories, 0g protein, 20g carbohydrates, 2g fat, 3g fiber, 0mg cholesterol, 0mg sodium, 150mg potassium.

Tomato and Cheese Breakfast Bake

Yield: 3 servings

Prep Time: 5 minutes

Cook Time: 12 minutes

Temperature: 350°F (175°C)

Cooking method: Bake

INGREDIENTS

- 3 large eggs
- 1/2 cup diced tomatoes
- 1/4 cup shredded mozzarella cheese
- 1/4 tsp dried oregano
- Salt and pepper, to taste

DIRECTIONS

1. Preheat the air fryer to 350°F (175°C).
2. In a bowl, whisk the eggs and mix in diced tomatoes, mozzarella cheese, oregano, salt, and pepper.
3. Pour the mixture into a greased baking dish that fits into your air fryer basket.
4. Bake for 12 minutes or until the eggs are set.
5. Allow to cool slightly before slicing and serving.

Nutritional Information

110 calories, 8g protein, 2g carbohydrates, 8g fat, 0g fiber, 180mg cholesterol, 150mg sodium, 120mg potassium.

Banana Oat Breakfast Bars

Yield: 6 servings   **Prep Time:** 5 minutes   **Cook Time:** 10 minutes   **Temperature:** 350°F (175°C)   **Cooking method:** Bake

INGREDIENTS

- 2 ripe bananas, mashed
- 1 cup rolled oats
- 1/4 cup chopped nuts (optional)
- 1 tbsp honey
- 1/2 tsp ground cinnamon

DIRECTIONS

1. Preheat the air fryer to 350°F (175°C).
2. In a bowl, mix mashed bananas, oats, nuts (if using), honey, and cinnamon.
3. Spread the mixture evenly in a greased baking dish that fits in the air fryer basket.
4. Bake for 10 minutes or until firm and lightly golden.
5. Let cool before cutting into bars.

Nutritional Information

110 calories, 2g protein, 18g carbohydrates, 4g fat, 2g fiber, 0mg cholesterol, 5mg sodium, 120mg potassium.

Chapter 3: Fast and Easy for Daily Use

Lemon Garlic Chicken Thighs

 Yield:
4 servings

 Prep Time:
5 minutes

 Cook Time:
15 minutes

Temperature:
375°F (190°C)

 Cooking method:
Fry

INGREDIENTS

- 4 bone-in, skin-on chicken thighs
- 2 tbsp lemon juice
- 1 tbsp olive oil
- 2 garlic cloves, minced
- Salt and pepper, to taste

DIRECTIONS

1. Preheat the air fryer to 375°F (190°C).
2. Rub chicken thighs with lemon juice, olive oil, garlic, salt, and pepper.
3. Place in the air fryer basket and cook for 15 minutes, flipping halfway through.
4. Serve hot.

Nutritional Information

210 calories, 18g protein, 1g carbohydrates, 15g fat, 0g fiber, 90mg cholesterol, 300mg sodium, 250mg potassium.

Zucchini Fritters

 Yield:
4 servings

 Prep Time:
10 minutes

Cook Time:
10 minutes

Temperature:
360°F (180°C)

Cooking method:
Fry

INGREDIENTS

- 2 medium zucchinis, grated
- 1/4 cup all-purpose flour
- 1 egg
- 1/4 tsp black pepper
- 1/4 tsp salt

DIRECTIONS

1. Preheat the air fryer to 360°F (180°C).
2. Mix grated zucchini, flour, egg, salt, and pepper in a bowl.
3. Form small patties and place in the air fryer basket.
4. Cook for 10 minutes or until golden brown, flipping halfway through.
5. Serve warm.

Nutritional Information

80 calories, 4g protein, 10g carbohydrates, 3g fat, 2g fiber, 40mg cholesterol, 180mg sodium, 250mg potassium.

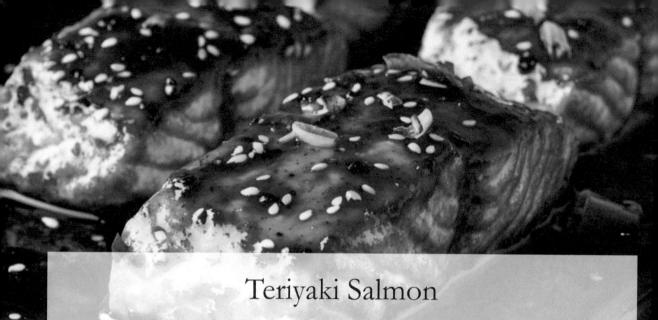

Teriyaki Salmon

 Yield:
4 servings

 Prep Time:
5 minutes

 Cook Time:
10 minutes

Temperature:
390°F (200°C)

 Cooking method:
Roast

INGREDIENTS

- 4 salmon fillets (4 oz each)
- 1/4 cup low-sodium teriyaki sauce
- 1 tbsp honey
- 1 tsp grated ginger

DIRECTIONS

1. Preheat the air fryer to 390°F (200°C).
2. Mix teriyaki sauce, honey, and ginger in a bowl.
3. Brush salmon fillets with the mixture and place them in the air fryer basket.
4. Cook for 10 minutes or until fully cooked.
5. Serve immediately.

Nutritional Information

210 calories, 22g protein, 10g carbohydrates, 9g fat, 0g fiber,
55mg cholesterol, 280mg sodium, 400mg potassium.

Sweet Potato Fries

 Yield:
4 servings

 Prep Time:
5 minutes

 Cook Time:
15 minutes

Temperature:
400°F (200°C)

 Cooking method:
Roast

INGREDIENTS

- 2 large sweet potatoes, cut into fries
- 1 tbsp olive oil
- 1/2 tsp smoked paprika
- Salt, to taste

DIRECTIONS

1. Preheat the air fryer to 400°F (200°C).
2. Toss sweet potato fries with olive oil, smoked paprika, and salt.
3. Place in the air fryer basket and roast for 15 minutes, shaking halfway through.
4. Serve hot.

Nutritional Information

120 calories, 2g protein, 28g carbohydrates, 3g fat, 4g fiber, 0mg cholesterol, 150mg sodium, 350mg potassium.

Garlic Parmesan Brussels Sprouts

 Yield:
4 servings

 Prep Time:
5 minutes

 Cook Time:
12 minutes

Temperature:
380°F (195°C)

Cooking method:
Roast

INGREDIENTS

- 1 lb Brussels sprouts, halved
- 1 tbsp olive oil
- 1/4 cup grated Parmesan cheese
- 1/2 tsp garlic powder
- Salt and pepper, to taste

DIRECTIONS

1. Preheat the air fryer to 380°F (195°C).
2. Toss Brussels sprouts with olive oil, Parmesan cheese, garlic powder, salt, and pepper.
3. Place in the air fryer basket and roast for 12 minutes, shaking halfway through.
4. Serve immediately.

Nutritional Information
110 calories, 5g protein, 10g carbohydrates, 6g fat, 3g fiber, 5mg cholesterol, 160mg sodium, 340mg potassium.

Buffalo Cauliflower Bites

Yield: 4 servings	Prep Time: 5 minutes	Cook Time: 10 minutes	Temperature: 375°F (190°C)	Cooking method: Fry

INGREDIENTS

- 1 head cauliflower, cut into florets
- 1/4 cup hot sauce
- 1 tbsp melted butter
- 1/2 tsp garlic powder

DIRECTIONS

1. Preheat the air fryer to 375°F (190°C).
2. In a bowl, toss the cauliflower florets with hot sauce, melted butter, and garlic powder.
3. Place in the air fryer basket and cook for 10 minutes, shaking halfway through.
4. Serve immediately.

Nutritional Information

90 calories, 3g protein, 8g carbohydrates, 5g fat, 3g fiber, 0mg cholesterol, 300mg sodium, 300mg potassium.

Chicken Fajitas

 Yield:
4 servings

 Prep Time:
5 minutes

 Cook Time:
15 minutes

 Temperature:
390°F (200°C)

 Cooking method:
Roast

INGREDIENTS

- 1 lb chicken breast, sliced
- 1 red bell pepper, sliced
- 1 green bell pepper, sliced
- 1 onion, sliced
- 1 tbsp olive oil
- 1 tsp chili powder
- Salt and pepper, to taste

DIRECTIONS

1. Preheat the air fryer to 390°F (200°C).
2. Toss the chicken, bell peppers, and onion with olive oil, chili powder, salt, and pepper.
3. Place the mixture in the air fryer basket and cook for 15 minutes, shaking halfway through.
4. Serve in tortillas if desired.

Nutritional Information

210 calories, 27g protein, 8g carbohydrates, 7g fat, 2g fiber,

70mg cholesterol, 200mg sodium, 400mg potassium.

Roasted Carrots

 Yield:
4 servings

 Prep Time:
5 minutes

 Cook Time:
12 minutes

 Temperature:
375°F (190°C)

 Cooking method:
Roast

INGREDIENTS

- 1 lb baby carrots
- 1 tbsp olive oil
- 1 tsp honey
- Salt and pepper, to taste

DIRECTIONS

1. Preheat the air fryer to 375°F (190°C).
2. In a bowl, mix carrots, olive oil, honey, salt, and pepper.
3. Place in the air fryer basket and roast for 12 minutes, shaking halfway through.
4. Serve warm.

Nutritional Information

80 calories, 1g protein, 12g carbohydrates, 3g fat, 3g fiber, 0mg cholesterol, 150mg sodium, 300mg potassium.

Turkey Meatballs

Yield:
4 servings

Prep Time:
10 minutes

Cook Time:
10 minutes

Temperature:
380°F (195°C)

Cooking method:
Fry

INGREDIENTS

- 1 lb ground turkey
- 1/4 cup breadcrumbs
- 1 egg
- 1/2 tsp garlic powder
- 1/2 tsp onion powder
- Salt and pepper, to taste

DIRECTIONS

1. Preheat the air fryer to 380°F (195°C).
2. In a bowl, mix ground turkey, breadcrumbs, egg, garlic powder, onion powder, salt, and pepper.
3. Form into small meatballs and place in the air fryer basket.
4. Cook for 10 minutes, shaking halfway through.
5. Serve hot.

Nutritional Information

120 calories, 15g protein, 3g carbohydrates, 6g fat, 0g fiber,
50mg cholesterol, 200mg sodium, 200mg potassium.

Stuffed Bell Peppers

Yield: 4 servings	Prep Time: 10 minutes	Cook Time: 15 minutes	Temperature: 360°F (180°C)	Cooking method: Bake

INGREDIENTS

- 4 bell peppers, tops cut off and seeded
- 1/2 lb lean ground beef
- 1/2 cup cooked rice
- 1/2 cup canned diced tomatoes
- 1/2 tsp dried oregano
- Salt and pepper, to taste

DIRECTIONS

1. Preheat the air fryer to 360°F (180°C).
2. In a bowl, mix ground beef, rice, diced tomatoes, oregano, salt, and pepper.
3. Stuff each bell pepper with the mixture and place in the air fryer basket.
4. Cook for 15 minutes or until the peppers are tender.
5. Serve warm.

Nutritional Information

180 calories, 15g protein, 14g carbohydrates, 7g fat, 3g fiber, 30mg cholesterol, 180mg sodium, 350mg potassium.

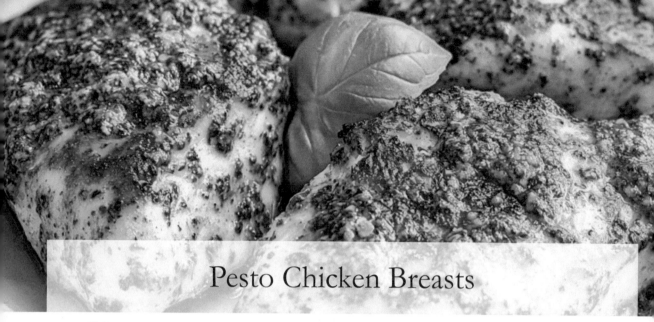

Pesto Chicken Breasts

Yield: 4 servings

Prep Time: 5 minutes

Cook Time: 15 minutes

Temperature: 375°F (190°C)

Cooking method: Bake

INGREDIENTS

- 4 boneless, skinless chicken breasts
- 1/4 cup basil pesto
- Salt and pepper, to taste

DIRECTIONS

1. Preheat the air fryer to 375°F (190°C).
2. Rub each chicken breast with basil pesto, ensuring they are evenly coated.
3. Place chicken breasts in the air fryer basket and cook for 15 minutes, flipping halfway through.
4. Ensure the internal temperature of the chicken reaches 165°F (74°C) before serving.

Nutritional Information

200 calories, 30g protein, 1g carbohydrates, 9g fat, 0g fiber, 75mg cholesterol, 250mg sodium, 350mg potassium.

Chickpea Salad

| Yield: 4 servings | Prep Time: 5 minutes | Cook Time: 15 minutes | Temperature: 400°F (200°C) | Cooking method: Roast |

INGREDIENTS

- 1 can (15 oz) chickpeas, drained and rinsed
- 1 tbsp olive oil
- 1/2 tsp paprika
- 1/2 tsp garlic powder
- Salt and pepper, to taste
- 1 cup cherry tomatoes, halved
- 1/4 cup chopped cucumber
- 1/4 cup crumbled feta cheese

DIRECTIONS

1. Preheat the air fryer to 400°F (200°C).
2. Toss chickpeas with olive oil, paprika, garlic powder, salt, and pepper.
3. Place chickpeas in the air fryer basket and roast for 15 minutes or until crispy, shaking halfway through.
4. In a bowl, mix roasted chickpeas, cherry tomatoes, cucumber, and feta. Serve immediately.

Nutritional Information

150 calories, 6g protein, 20g carbohydrates, 7g fat, 5g fiber, 5mg cholesterol, 250mg sodium, 200mg potassium.

Shrimp Tacos

 Yield:
4 servings

 Prep Time:
5 minutes

 Cook Time:
8 minutes

 Temperature:
375°F (190°C)

 Cooking method:
Fry

INGREDIENTS

- 1 lb shrimp, peeled and deveined
- 1 tbsp olive oil
- 1 tsp smoked paprika
- 1/2 tsp ground cumin
- Salt and pepper, to taste
- 8 small corn tortillas
- 1/2 cup shredded cabbage

DIRECTIONS

1. Preheat the air fryer to 375°F (190°C).
2. Toss shrimp with olive oil, smoked paprika, cumin, salt, and pepper.
3. Place shrimp in the air fryer basket and fry for 8 minutes, shaking halfway through.
4. Serve shrimp in corn tortillas with shredded cabbage.

Nutritional Information

180 calories, 20g protein, 18g carbohydrates, 6g fat, 2g fiber,
150mg cholesterol, 280mg sodium, 250mg potassium.

Cabbage Steaks

 Yield:
4 servings

 Prep Time:
5 minutes

 Cook Time:
15 minutes

 Temperature:
375°F (190°C)

 Cooking method:
Roast

INGREDIENTS

- 1 head of cabbage, sliced into 1-inch thick steaks
- 2 tbsp olive oil
- 1 tsp garlic powder
- Salt and pepper, to taste

DIRECTIONS

1. Preheat the air fryer to 375°F (190°C).
2. Brush cabbage steaks with olive oil, then sprinkle with garlic powder, salt, and pepper.
3. Place cabbage steaks in the air fryer basket and roast for 15 minutes, flipping halfway through.
4. Serve warm.

Nutritional Information

90 calories, 1g protein, 9g carbohydrates, 7g fat, 4g fiber, 0mg cholesterol, 100mg sodium, 300mg potassium.

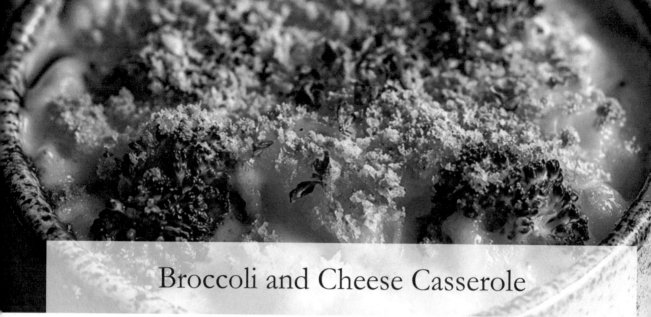

Broccoli and Cheese Casserole

 Yield:
4 servings

 Prep Time:
5 minutes

 Cook Time:
12 minutes

🌡 Temperature:
350°F (175°C)

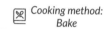 Cooking method:
Bake

INGREDIENTS

- 3 cups broccoli florets
- 1/2 cup shredded cheddar cheese
- 1/4 cup low-fat milk
- 1/2 tsp garlic powder
- Salt and pepper, to taste

DIRECTIONS

1. Preheat the air fryer to 350°F (175°C).
2. In a bowl, mix broccoli, shredded cheddar cheese, milk, garlic powder, salt, and pepper.
3. Transfer the mixture to a baking dish that fits in the air fryer basket.
4. Bake in the air fryer for 12 minutes or until the cheese is melted and bubbly.
5. Serve warm.

Nutritional Information

130 calories, 6g protein, 8g carbohydrates, 8g fat, 2g fiber, 15mg cholesterol, 180mg sodium, 300mg potassium.

Chapter 4: Best for Couple

Lemon Herb Salmon

 Yield:
2 servings

 Prep Time:
5 minutes

Cook Time:
10 minutes

Temperature:
400°F (200°C)

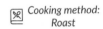 Cooking method:
Roast

INGREDIENTS

- 2 salmon fillets (4 oz each)
- 1 tbsp lemon juice
- 1 tsp olive oil
- 1/2 tsp dried oregano
- Salt and pepper, to taste

DIRECTIONS

1. Preheat the air fryer to 400°F (200°C).
2. Drizzle salmon fillets with lemon juice and olive oil. Season with dried oregano, salt, and pepper.
3. Place salmon fillets in the air fryer basket and roast for 10 minutes or until fully cooked.
4. Serve with lemon wedges.

Nutritional Information

210 calories, 22g protein, 1g carbohydrates, 12g fat, 0g fiber, 55mg cholesterol, 150mg sodium, 450mg potassium.

Garlic Butter Shrimp

Yield:
2 servings

Prep Time:
5 minutes

Cook Time:
8 minutes

Temperature:
375°F (190°C)

Cooking method:
Fry

INGREDIENTS

- 1/2 lb shrimp, peeled and deveined
- 2 tbsp melted butter
- 2 garlic cloves, minced
- 1/2 tsp smoked paprika
- Salt and pepper, to taste

DIRECTIONS

1. Preheat the air fryer to 375°F (190°C).
2. Toss shrimp with melted butter, minced garlic, smoked paprika, salt, and pepper.
3. Place shrimp in the air fryer basket and cook for 8 minutes, shaking halfway through.
4. Serve hot with a side of your choice.

Nutritional Information

190 calories, 20g protein, 1g carbohydrates, 13g fat, 0g fiber,

160mg cholesterol, 250mg sodium, 300mg potassium.

Chicken Parmesan

 Yield:
2 servings

 Prep Time:
5 minutes

 Cook Time:
12 minutes

Temperature:
375°F (190°C)

 Cooking method:
Bake

INGREDIENTS

- 2 boneless, skinless chicken breasts (4 oz each)
- 1/4 cup marinara sauce
- 1/4 cup grated Parmesan cheese
- 1/2 cup panko breadcrumbs
- 1/2 tsp Italian seasoning
- Cooking spray

DIRECTIONS

1. Preheat the air fryer to 375°F (190°C).
2. Mix panko breadcrumbs and Italian seasoning in a shallow dish. Coat each chicken breast in the mixture.
3. Spray the air fryer basket with cooking spray and place the chicken breasts inside. Cook for 10 minutes.
4. Spoon marinara sauce over the chicken and top with Parmesan cheese. Cook for an additional 2 minutes until the cheese melts.
5. Serve immediately.

Nutritional Information

270 calories, 34g protein, 12g carbohydrates, 10g fat, 1g fiber, 80mg cholesterol, 400mg sodium, 300mg potassium.

Veggie Stuffed Mushrooms

Yield: 2 servings

Prep Time: 5 minutes

Cook Time: 10 minutes

Temperature: 350°F (175°C)

Cooking method: Bake

INGREDIENTS

- 6 large button mushrooms, stems removed
- 1/4 cup diced bell pepper
- 2 tbsp chopped onion
- 2 tbsp grated mozzarella cheese
- 1 tsp olive oil
- Salt and pepper, to taste

DIRECTIONS

1. Preheat the air fryer to 350°F (175°C).
2. In a bowl, mix diced bell pepper, onion, olive oil, salt, and pepper. Fill the mushroom caps with the mixture.
3. Place stuffed mushrooms in the air fryer basket and bake for 10 minutes.
4. Sprinkle with grated mozzarella cheese and bake for an additional 2 minutes.
5. Serve warm.

Nutritional Information

110 calories, 3g protein, 6g carbohydrates, 8g fat, 1g fiber, 5mg cholesterol, 90mg sodium, 150mg potassium.

Pork Tenderloin with Apples

 Yield:
2 servings

 Prep Time:
5 minutes

 Cook Time:
15 minutes

 Temperature:
375°F (190°C)

 Cooking method:
Roast

INGREDIENTS

- 8 oz pork tenderloin
- 1 medium apple, cored and sliced
- 1 tbsp honey
- 1/2 tsp ground cinnamon
- 1 tsp olive oil
- Salt and pepper, to taste

DIRECTIONS

1. Preheat the air fryer to 375°F (190°C).
2. Rub the pork tenderloin with olive oil, salt, and pepper. Toss apple slices with honey and cinnamon.
3. Place the pork tenderloin and apple slices in the air fryer basket.
4. Roast for 15 minutes or until the pork reaches an internal temperature of 145°F (63°C), flipping halfway through.
5. Slice the pork and serve with apples.

Nutritional Information

250 calories, 25g protein, 18g carbohydrates, 10g fat, 2g fiber,

75mg cholesterol, 150mg sodium, 300mg potassium.

Lemon Butter Cod

Yield: 2 servings	Prep Time: 5 minutes	Cook Time: 10 minutes	Temperature: 375°F (190°C)	Cooking method: Roast

INGREDIENTS

- 2 cod fillets (6 oz each)
- 1 tbsp melted butter
- 1 tbsp lemon juice
- 1/2 tsp garlic powder
- Salt and pepper, to taste

DIRECTIONS

1. Preheat the air fryer to 375°F (190°C).
2. In a bowl, mix melted butter, lemon juice, garlic powder, salt, and pepper.
3. Brush the cod fillets with the lemon butter mixture and place them in the air fryer basket.
4. Roast for 10 minutes or until the cod flakes easily with a fork.
5. Serve with lemon wedges.

Nutritional Information

180 calories, 30g protein, 1g carbohydrates, 6g fat, 0g fiber, 80mg cholesterol, 300mg sodium, 400mg potassium.

Garlic Lemon Shrimp Skewers

 Yield: 4 servings   **Prep Time:** 10 minutes   **Cook Time:** 8 minutes   **Temperature:** 375°F (190°C)   **Cooking method:** Fry

INGREDIENTS

- 1 lb shrimp, peeled and deveined
- 1 tbsp olive oil
- 1 tbsp lemon juice
- 2 garlic cloves, minced
- 1/2 tsp smoked paprika
- Salt and pepper, to taste

DIRECTIONS

1. Preheat the air fryer to 375°F (190°C).
2. Toss shrimp with olive oil, lemon juice, minced garlic, smoked paprika, salt, and pepper.
3. Thread the shrimp onto skewers and place them in the air fryer basket.
4. Fry for 8 minutes, flipping halfway through.
5. Serve with a lemon wedge.

Nutritional Information

150 calories, 25g protein, 2g carbohydrates, 5g fat, 0g fiber, 180mg cholesterol, 200mg sodium, 300mg potassium.

Cajun Mahi-Mahi

 Yield:
2 servings

 Prep Time:
5 minutes

 Cook Time:
10 minutes

 Temperature:
380°F (195°C)

 Cooking method:
Roast

INGREDIENTS

- 2 mahi-mahi fillets (6 oz each)
- 1 tbsp olive oil
- 1 tsp Cajun seasoning
- Salt, to taste

DIRECTIONS

1. Preheat the air fryer to 380°F (195°C).
2. Brush the mahi-mahi fillets with olive oil and season with Cajun seasoning and salt.
3. Place the fillets in the air fryer basket and roast for 10 minutes or until cooked through.
4. Serve immediately.

Nutritional Information

200 calories, 30g protein, 1g carbohydrates, 8g fat, 0g fiber, 85mg cholesterol, 250mg sodium, 350mg potassium.

Crispy Fish Tacos

 Yield:
4 servings

 Prep Time:
10 minutes

 Cook Time:
12 minutes

 Temperature:
400°F (200°C)

 Cooking method:
Fry

INGREDIENTS

- 4 white fish fillets (4 oz each, such as tilapia or cod)
- 1/2 cup panko breadcrumbs
- 1 tsp smoked paprika
- 1/2 tsp garlic powder
- Salt and pepper, to taste
- 8 small corn tortillas
- 1 cup shredded cabbage

DIRECTIONS

1. Preheat the air fryer to 400°F (200°C).
2. In a shallow dish, mix panko breadcrumbs, smoked paprika, garlic powder, salt, and pepper.
3. Coat each fish fillet with the breadcrumb mixture and place in the air fryer basket.
4. Fry for 12 minutes or until crispy and fully cooked, flipping halfway through.
5. Serve fish in tortillas with shredded cabbage.

Nutritional Information

250 calories, 25g protein, 25g carbohydrates, 6g fat, 3g fiber, 50mg cholesterol, 300mg sodium, 350mg potassium.

Lemon Dill Salmon

 Yield:
2 servings

 Prep Time:
5 minutes

 Cook Time:
10 minutes

 Temperature:
375°F (190°C)

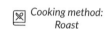 *Cooking method:*
Roast

INGREDIENTS

- 2 salmon fillets (6 oz each)
- 1 tbsp lemon juice
- 1/2 tsp dried dill
- 1 tsp olive oil
- Salt and pepper, to taste

DIRECTIONS

1. Preheat the air fryer to 375°F (190°C).
2. Brush the salmon fillets with lemon juice and olive oil. Sprinkle with dried dill, salt, and pepper.
3. Place the salmon fillets in the air fryer basket and roast for 10 minutes or until cooked through.
4. Serve with additional lemon wedges.

Nutritional Information

220 calories, 25g protein, 1g carbohydrates, 12g fat, 0g fiber,
55mg cholesterol, 250mg sodium, 400mg potassium.

Chapter 6: Meat: Beef, Pork, Lamb and Poultry

Lemon Herb Chicken Thighs

 Yield:
4 servings

 Prep Time:
5 minutes

 Cook Time:
15 minutes

 Temperature:
375°F (190°C)

 Cooking method:
Roast

INGREDIENTS

- 4 bone-in, skin-on chicken thighs
- 1 tbsp lemon juice
- 1 tbsp olive oil
- 1 tsp dried oregano
- Salt and pepper, to taste

DIRECTIONS

1. Preheat the air fryer to 375°F (190°C).
2. Rub chicken thighs with lemon juice, olive oil, dried oregano, salt, and pepper.
3. Place in the air fryer basket and roast for 15 minutes, flipping halfway through.
4. Serve hot.

Nutritional Information

210 calories, 18g protein, 1g carbohydrates, 15g fat, 0g fiber,
75mg cholesterol, 300mg sodium, 350mg potassium.

Garlic Butter Pork Chops

 Yield:
4 servings

 Prep Time:
5 minutes

 Cook Time:
12 minutes

 Temperature:
380°F (195°C)

 Cooking method:
Fry

INGREDIENTS

- 4 boneless pork chops (6 oz each)
- 2 tbsp melted butter
- 2 garlic cloves, minced
- 1/2 tsp dried thyme
- Salt and pepper, to taste

DIRECTIONS

1. Preheat the air fryer to 380°F (195°C).
2. Brush pork chops with melted butter and minced garlic. Season with dried thyme, salt, and pepper.
3. Place in the air fryer basket and fry for 12 minutes, flipping halfway through.
4. Serve hot.

Nutritional Information

240 calories, 25g protein, 1g carbohydrates, 14g fat, 0g fiber,
65mg cholesterol, 300mg sodium, 400mg potassium.

Honey Mustard Chicken Drumsticks

 Yield:
4 servings

 Prep Time:
5 minutes

 Cook Time:
18 minutes

Temperature:
375°F (190°C)

 Cooking method:
Fry

INGREDIENTS

- 8 chicken drumsticks
- 1 tbsp honey
- 1 tbsp Dijon mustard
- 1/2 tsp garlic powder
- Salt and pepper, to taste

DIRECTIONS

1. Preheat the air fryer to 375°F (190°C).
2. Mix honey, Dijon mustard, garlic powder, salt, and pepper. Brush onto the chicken drumsticks.
3. Place in the air fryer basket and fry for 18 minutes, flipping halfway through.
4. Serve warm.

Nutritional Information

220 calories, 20g protein, 6g carbohydrates, 12g fat, 0g fiber, 90mg cholesterol, 350mg sodium, 250mg potassium.

Spiced Lamb Chops

Yield: 4 servings

Prep Time: 5 minutes

Cook Time: 10 minutes

Temperature: 400°F (200°C)

Cooking method: Roast

INGREDIENTS

- 8 lamb chops
- 1 tbsp olive oil
- 1 tsp ground cumin

- 1/2 tsp smoked paprika
- Salt and pepper, to taste

DIRECTIONS

1. Preheat the air fryer to 400°F (200°C).
2. Rub lamb chops with olive oil, ground cumin, smoked paprika, salt, and pepper.
3. Place in the air fryer basket and roast for 10 minutes, flipping halfway through.
4. Serve hot.

Nutritional Information

290 calories, 25g protein, 1g carbohydrates, 21g fat, 0g fiber, 80mg cholesterol, 300mg sodium, 400mg potassium.

BBQ Chicken Breasts

 Yield:
4 servings

 Prep Time:
5 minutes

 Cook Time:
12 minutes

Temperature:
380°F (195°C)

 Cooking method:
Fry

INGREDIENTS

- 4 boneless, skinless chicken breasts (4 oz each)
- 1/4 cup BBQ sauce
- Salt and pepper, to taste

DIRECTIONS

1. Preheat the air fryer to 380°F (195°C).
2. Season the chicken breasts with salt and pepper. Brush both sides with BBQ sauce.
3. Place in the air fryer basket and fry for 12 minutes, flipping halfway through.
4. Serve hot.

Nutritional Information

180 calories, 28g protein, 5g carbohydrates, 4g fat, 0g fiber,

75mg cholesterol, 300mg sodium, 300mg potassium.

Teriyaki Beef Skewers

 Yield:
4 servings

 Prep Time:
10 minutes

 Cook Time:
10 minutes

 Temperature:
400°F (200°C)

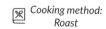 Cooking method:
Roast

INGREDIENTS

- 1 lb beef sirloin, cut into 1-inch cubes
- 1/4 cup low-sodium teriyaki sauce
- 1 tbsp olive oil
- 1/2 tsp ground ginger

DIRECTIONS

1. Preheat the air fryer to 400°F (200°C).
2. Toss beef cubes with teriyaki sauce, olive oil, and ground ginger. Thread onto skewers.
3. Place skewers in the air fryer basket and roast for 10 minutes, flipping halfway through.
4. Serve with additional teriyaki sauce.

Nutritional Information

210 calories, 24g protein, 4g carbohydrates, 11g fat, 0g fiber,
60mg cholesterol, 450mg sodium, 300mg potassium.

Herb-Crusted Pork Tenderloin

 Yield:
4 servings

 Prep Time:
5 minutes

 Cook Time:
15 minutes

 Temperature:
375°F (190°C)

 **Cooking method:**
Roast

INGREDIENTS

- 1 lb pork tenderloin
- 1 tbsp olive oil
- 1 tsp dried rosemary
- 1/2 tsp garlic powder
- Salt and pepper, to taste

DIRECTIONS

1. Preheat the air fryer to 375°F (190°C).
2. Rub pork tenderloin with olive oil, rosemary, garlic powder, salt, and pepper.
3. Place in the air fryer basket and roast for 15 minutes or until internal temperature reaches 145°F (63°C).
4. Allow to rest for 5 minutes before slicing.

Nutritional Information

200 calories, 28g protein, 1g carbohydrates, 9g fat, 0g fiber, 75mg cholesterol, 300mg sodium, 400mg potassium.

Lemon Garlic Lamb Koftas

 Yield:
4 servings

 Prep Time:
10 minutes

 Cook Time:
12 minutes

 Temperature:
375°F (190°C)

 **Cooking method:**
Fry

INGREDIENTS

- 1 lb ground lamb
- 2 garlic cloves, minced
- 1 tbsp lemon juice
- 1 tsp ground cumin
- Salt and pepper, to taste

DIRECTIONS

1. Preheat the air fryer to 375°F (190°C).
2. Mix ground lamb, minced garlic, lemon juice, ground cumin, salt, and pepper.
3. Form the mixture into 8 small koftas.
4. Place in the air fryer basket and fry for 12 minutes, flipping halfway through.
5. Serve with a side of yogurt sauce.

Nutritional Information

260 calories, 22g protein, 2g carbohydrates, 18g fat, 0g fiber,
65mg cholesterol, 250mg sodium, 300mg potassium.

Honey Soy Chicken Wings

 Yield:
4 servings

 Prep Time:
5 minutes

 Cook Time:
20 minutes

Temperature:
400°F (200°C)

 Cooking method:
Fry

INGREDIENTS

- 2 lbs chicken wings
- 2 tbsp honey
- 2 tbsp soy sauce (low sodium)
- 1/2 tsp garlic powder

DIRECTIONS

1. Preheat the air fryer to 400°F (200°C).
2. Mix honey, soy sauce, and garlic powder in a bowl. Toss the chicken wings in the mixture until evenly coated.
3. Place in the air fryer basket and fry for 20 minutes, shaking halfway through.
4. Serve immediately.

Nutritional Information

220 calories, 18g protein, 8g carbohydrates, 13g fat, 0g fiber, 70mg cholesterol, 500mg sodium, 250mg potassium.

BBQ Pulled Pork

 Yield:
4 servings

 Prep Time:
5 minutes

 Cook Time:
25 minutes

 *Temperature:*
350°F (175°C)

Cooking method:
Roast

INGREDIENTS

- 1 lb pork shoulder, trimmed and cut into chunks
- 1/4 cup BBQ sauce
- 1 tsp smoked paprika
- Salt and pepper, to taste

DIRECTIONS

1. Preheat the air fryer to 350°F (175°C).
2. Rub pork shoulder chunks with smoked paprika, salt, and pepper. Place in the air fryer basket.
3. Roast for 20 minutes. Add BBQ sauce, stir, and cook for an additional 5 minutes.
4. Shred pork with a fork before serving.

Nutritional Information

Calories: 300, Protein: 25g, Carbohydrates: 12g, Fat: 18g, Fiber: 1g, Sodium: 600mg, Potassium: 350mg, Cholesterol: 85mg, Calories: 300

Herb-Marinated Chicken Breast

 Yield:
4 servings

 Prep Time:
10 minutes

 Cook Time:
15 minutes

Temperature:
375°F (190°C)

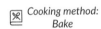 Cooking method:
Bake

INGREDIENTS

- 4 boneless, skinless chicken breasts (4 oz each)
- 1/4 cup olive oil
- 1 tbsp lemon juice
- 1 tsp dried basil
- 1 tsp dried thyme
- Salt and pepper, to taste

DIRECTIONS

1. Preheat the air fryer to 375°F (190°C).
2. In a bowl, whisk together olive oil, lemon juice, dried basil, thyme, salt, and pepper. Coat the chicken breasts in the mixture.
3. Place chicken breasts in the air fryer basket and bake for 15 minutes, flipping halfway through.
4. Serve immediately.

Nutritional Information

220 calories, 28g protein, 1g carbohydrates, 10g fat, 0g fiber,

75mg cholesterol, 200mg sodium, 350mg potassium.

Spicy Beef Meatballs

 Yield:
4 servings

 Prep Time:
10 minutes

 Cook Time:
12 minutes

Temperature:
380°F (195°C)

Cooking method:
Fry

INGREDIENTS

- 1 lb lean ground beef
- 1/4 cup breadcrumbs
- 1 egg

- 1 tsp chili powder
- 1/2 tsp garlic powder
- Salt and pepper, to taste

DIRECTIONS

1. Preheat the air fryer to 380°F (195°C).
2. In a bowl, mix ground beef, breadcrumbs, egg, chili powder, garlic powder, salt, and pepper.
3. Form into small meatballs and place them in the air fryer basket.
4. Fry for 12 minutes, shaking halfway through.
5. Serve hot.

Nutritional Information

180 calories, 18g protein, 4g carbohydrates, 10g fat, 0g fiber,
60mg cholesterol, 150mg sodium, 300mg potassium.

Rosemary Lamb Shoulder Chops

 Yield:
4 servings

 Prep Time:
5 minutes

 Cook Time:
15 minutes

Temperature:
400°F (200°C)

 Cooking method:
Roast

INGREDIENTS

- 4 lamb shoulder chops
- 2 tbsp olive oil
- 1 tsp dried rosemary
- 1/2 tsp garlic powder
- Salt and pepper, to taste

DIRECTIONS

1. Preheat the air fryer to 400°F (200°C).
2. Rub the lamb chops with olive oil, rosemary, garlic powder, salt, and pepper.
3. Place in the air fryer basket and roast for 15 minutes, flipping halfway through.
4. Serve warm.

Nutritional Information

290 calories, 24g protein, 1g carbohydrates, 22g fat, 0g fiber,
75mg cholesterol, 250mg sodium, 400mg potassium.

Ginger Soy Chicken Thighs

Yield: 4 servings

Prep Time: 10 minutes

Cook Time: 18 minutes

Temperature: 375°F (190°C)

Cooking method: Bake

INGREDIENTS

- 4 boneless, skinless chicken thighs
- 2 tbsp soy sauce (low sodium)
- 1 tbsp honey
- 1 tbsp grated ginger
- 1 garlic clove, minced

DIRECTIONS

1. Preheat the air fryer to 375°F (190°C).
2. In a bowl, mix soy sauce, honey, ginger, and garlic. Coat the chicken thighs in the marinade.
3. Place in the air fryer basket and bake for 18 minutes, flipping halfway through.
4. Serve hot.

Nutritional Information

210 calories, 22g protein, 6g carbohydrates, 10g fat, 0g fiber, 80mg cholesterol, 400mg sodium, 250mg potassium.

Pork Tenderloin Medallions

 Yield: 4 servings   **Prep Time:** 5 minutes   **Cook Time:** 10 minutes   **Temperature:** 375°F (190°C)   **Cooking method:** Roast

INGREDIENTS

- 1 lb pork tenderloin, cut into medallions
- 1 tbsp olive oil
- 1 tsp smoked paprika
- 1/2 tsp garlic powder
- Salt and pepper, to taste

DIRECTIONS

1. Preheat the air fryer to 375°F (190°C).
2. Coat the pork medallions with olive oil, smoked paprika, garlic powder, salt, and pepper.
3. Place in the air fryer basket and roast for 10 minutes, flipping halfway through.
4. Serve immediately.

Nutritional Information

200 calories, 26g protein, 1g carbohydrates, 9g fat, 0g fiber, 65mg cholesterol, 200mg sodium, 350mg potassium.

Chapter 7: Vegetarian Favourites

Zucchini Fritters

 Yield:
4 servings

 Prep Time:
10 minutes

 Cook Time:
10 minutes

 Temperature:
360°F (180°C)

Cooking method:
Fry

INGREDIENTS

- 2 medium zucchinis, grated
- 1/4 cup all-purpose flour
- 1 egg
- 1/4 tsp black pepper
- 1/4 tsp salt

DIRECTIONS

1. Preheat the air fryer to 360°F (180°C).
2. Mix grated zucchini, flour, egg, salt, and pepper in a bowl.
3. Form small patties and place in the air fryer basket.
4. Cook for 10 minutes or until golden brown, flipping halfway through.
5. Serve warm.

Nutritional Information

90 calories, 4g protein, 10g carbohydrates, 3g fat, 2g fiber, 40mg cholesterol, 180mg sodium, 250mg potassium.

Cauliflower Buffalo Bites

Yield:
4 servings

Prep Time:
5 minutes

Cook Time:
15 minutes

Temperature:
375°F (190°C)

Cooking method:
Fry

INGREDIENTS

- 1 head cauliflower, cut into florets
- 1/4 cup hot sauce
- 1 tbsp melted butter
- 1/2 tsp garlic powder

DIRECTIONS

1. Preheat the air fryer to 375°F (190°C).
2. In a bowl, toss the cauliflower florets with hot sauce, melted butter, and garlic powder.
3. Place in the air fryer basket and cook for 15 minutes, shaking halfway through.
4. Serve with a side of blue cheese dip if desired.

Nutritional Information

90 calories, 3g protein, 8g carbohydrates, 5g fat, 3g fiber, 0mg cholesterol, 300mg sodium, 300mg potassium.

Sweet Potato Wedges

| Yield: 4 servings | Prep Time: 5 minutes | Cook Time: 15 minutes | Temperature: 400°F (200°C) | Cooking method: Roast |

INGREDIENTS

- 2 large sweet potatoes, cut into wedges
- 1 tbsp olive oil
- 1/2 tsp smoked paprika
- Salt, to taste

DIRECTIONS

1. Preheat the air fryer to 400°F (200°C).
2. Toss the sweet potato wedges with olive oil, smoked paprika, and salt.
3. Place in the air fryer basket and roast for 15 minutes, shaking halfway through.
4. Serve hot.

Nutritional Information

120 calories, 2g protein, 28g carbohydrates, 3g fat, 4g fiber, 0mg cholesterol, 150mg sodium, 350mg potassium.

Crispy Tofu Bites

 Yield:
4 servings

 Prep Time:
10 minutes

 Cook Time:
12 minutes

🌡 Temperature:
375°F (190°C)

 Cooking method:
Fry

INGREDIENTS

- 1 block (14 oz) firm tofu, drained and cubed
- 1 tbsp soy sauce (low sodium)
- 1 tbsp cornstarch
- 1/2 tsp garlic powder

DIRECTIONS

1. Preheat the air fryer to 375°F (190°C).
2. Toss tofu cubes in soy sauce, cornstarch, and garlic powder until evenly coated.
3. Place tofu in the air fryer basket and cook for 12 minutes, shaking halfway through.
4. Serve with a dipping sauce of your choice.

Nutritional Information

120 calories, 10g protein, 5g carbohydrates, 7g fat, 1g fiber, 0mg cholesterol, 250mg sodium, 200mg potassium.

Stuffed Bell Peppers

 Yield:
4 servings

 Prep Time:
10 minutes

 Cook Time:
15 minutes

 Temperature:
360°F (180°C)

 Cooking method:
Bake

INGREDIENTS

- 4 bell peppers, tops cut off and seeds removed
- 1 cup cooked quinoa
- 1/2 cup canned black beans, drained and rinsed
- 1/2 cup diced tomatoes
- 1/2 tsp cumin
- Salt and pepper, to taste

DIRECTIONS

1. Preheat the air fryer to 360°F (180°C).
2. In a bowl, mix quinoa, black beans, diced tomatoes, cumin, salt, and pepper. Stuff the bell peppers with the mixture.
3. Place in the air fryer basket and bake for 15 minutes or until the peppers are tender.
4. Serve warm.

Nutritional Information

140 calories, 5g protein, 28g carbohydrates, 2g fat, 4g fiber, 0mg cholesterol, 180mg sodium, 300mg potassium.

Eggplant Parmesan

 Yield:
4 servings

 Prep Time:
10 minutes

 Cook Time:
15 minutes

Temperature:
375°F (190°C)

 Cooking method:
Bake

INGREDIENTS

- 1 medium eggplant, sliced into 1/2-inch rounds
- 1/2 cup breadcrumbs
- 1/4 cup grated Parmesan cheese
- 1/2 tsp Italian seasoning
- Cooking spray

DIRECTIONS

1. Preheat the air fryer to 375°F (190°C).
2. In a bowl, mix breadcrumbs, Parmesan cheese, and Italian seasoning.
3. Spray the eggplant slices with cooking spray and coat them in the breadcrumb mixture.
4. Place in the air fryer basket and bake for 15 minutes or until golden and crispy, flipping halfway through.
5. Serve with marinara sauce if desired.

Nutritional Information

130 calories, 5g protein, 16g carbohydrates, 6g fat, 4g fiber, 5mg cholesterol, 250mg sodium, 300mg potassium.

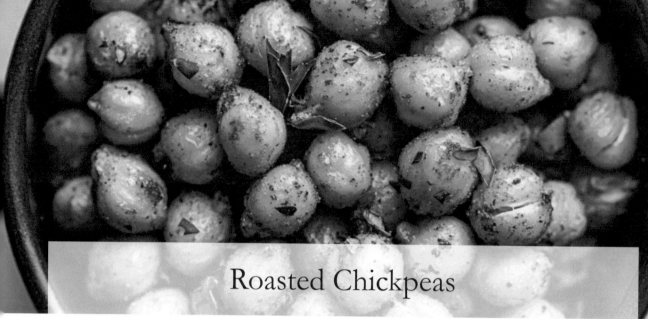

Roasted Chickpeas

 Yield:
4 servings

 Prep Time:
5 minutes

 Cook Time:
15 minutes

 Temperature:
400°F (200°C)

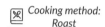 Cooking method:
Roast

INGREDIENTS

- 1 can (15 oz) chickpeas, drained and rinsed
- 1 tbsp olive oil
- 1/2 tsp smoked paprika
- 1/2 tsp garlic powder
- Salt, to taste

DIRECTIONS

1. Preheat the air fryer to 400°F (200°C).
2. Toss the chickpeas with olive oil, smoked paprika, garlic powder, and salt.
3. Place in the air fryer basket and roast for 15 minutes, shaking halfway through.
4. Serve as a snack or salad topping.

Nutritional Information

120 calories, 5g protein, 17g carbohydrates, 4g fat, 4g fiber, 0mg cholesterol, 240mg sodium, 250mg potassium.

Stuffed Mushrooms

 Yield:
4 servings

 Prep Time:
10 minutes

 Cook Time:
10 minutes

Temperature:
350°F (175°C)

 Cooking method:
Bake

INGREDIENTS

- 12 large button mushrooms, stems removed
- 1/4 cup cream cheese, softened
- 1/4 cup grated mozzarella cheese
- 2 tbsp chopped parsley
- 1 garlic clove, minced

DIRECTIONS

1. Preheat the air fryer to 350°F (175°C).
2. In a bowl, mix cream cheese, mozzarella cheese, parsley, and minced garlic.
3. Spoon the mixture into the mushroom caps.
4. Place stuffed mushrooms in the air fryer basket and bake for 10 minutes or until the cheese is bubbly.
5. Serve warm.

Nutritional Information

90 calories, 3g protein, 4g carbohydrates, 7g fat, 1g fiber, 15mg cholesterol, 150mg sodium, 200mg potassium.

Cauliflower Steaks

 Yield:
4 servings

 Prep Time:
5 minutes

 Cook Time:
15 minutes

 Temperature:
375°F (190°C)

Cooking method:
Roast

INGREDIENTS

- 1 large head cauliflower, sliced into 1-inch thick steaks
- 1 tbsp olive oil

- 1/2 tsp garlic powder
- 1/2 tsp smoked paprika
- Salt and pepper, to taste

DIRECTIONS

1. Preheat the air fryer to 375°F (190°C).
2. Brush the cauliflower steaks with olive oil and season with garlic powder, smoked paprika, salt, and pepper.
3. Place in the air fryer basket and roast for 15 minutes, flipping halfway through.
4. Serve warm.

Nutritional Information

70 calories, 2g protein, 6g carbohydrates, 5g fat, 3g fiber, 0mg cholesterol, 150mg sodium, 300mg potassium.

Spinach and Feta Stuffed Peppers

 Yield:
4 servings

 Prep Time:
10 minutes

 Cook Time:
15 minutes

 Temperature:
360°F (180°C)

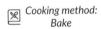 Cooking method:
Bake

INGREDIENTS

- 4 bell peppers, tops cut off and seeds removed
- 1 cup fresh spinach, chopped
- 1/2 cup crumbled feta cheese
- 1/4 cup cooked quinoa
- Salt and pepper, to taste

DIRECTIONS

1. Preheat the air fryer to 360°F (180°C).
2. In a bowl, mix chopped spinach, feta cheese, cooked quinoa, salt, and pepper. Stuff the bell peppers with the mixture.
3. Place in the air fryer basket and bake for 15 minutes or until the peppers are tender.
4. Serve warm.

Nutritional Information

130 calories, 4g protein, 15g carbohydrates, 6g fat, 3g fiber,
10mg cholesterol, 180mg sodium, 300mg potassium.

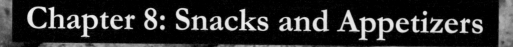

Chapter 8: Snacks and Appetizers

Mozzarella Sticks

 Yield:
4 servings

 Prep Time:
10 minutes

 Cook Time:
6 minutes

Temperature:
390°F (200°C)

 Cooking method:
Fry

INGREDIENTS

- 8 mozzarella cheese sticks
- 1/2 cup breadcrumbs
- 1/2 tsp Italian seasoning
- 1 egg, beaten
- Cooking spray

DIRECTIONS

1. Preheat the air fryer to 390°F (200°C).
2. Dip each cheese stick into the beaten egg, then coat with breadcrumbs mixed with Italian seasoning.
3. Place in the freezer for 30 minutes to set.
4. Spray the air fryer basket with cooking spray and place the mozzarella sticks inside. Cook for 6 minutes or until golden.
5. Serve with marinara sauce.

Nutritional Information

120 calories, 8g protein, 10g carbohydrates, 6g fat, 0g fiber,
30mg cholesterol, 250mg sodium, 100mg potassium.

Spicy Chickpeas

 Yield:
4 servings

 Prep Time:
5 minutes

 Cook Time:
15 minutes

Temperature:
400°F (200°C)

 Cooking method:
Roast

INGREDIENTS

- 1 can (15 oz) chickpeas, drained and rinsed
- 1 tbsp olive oil
- 1/2 tsp smoked paprika
- 1/2 tsp cayenne pepper
- Salt, to taste

DIRECTIONS

1. Preheat the air fryer to 400°F (200°C).
2. Toss the chickpeas with olive oil, smoked paprika, cayenne pepper, and salt.
3. Place in the air fryer basket and roast for 15 minutes, shaking halfway through.
4. Serve as a snack.

Nutritional Information

120 calories, 5g protein, 17g carbohydrates, 4g fat, 4g fiber, 0mg cholesterol, 240mg sodium, 250mg potassium.

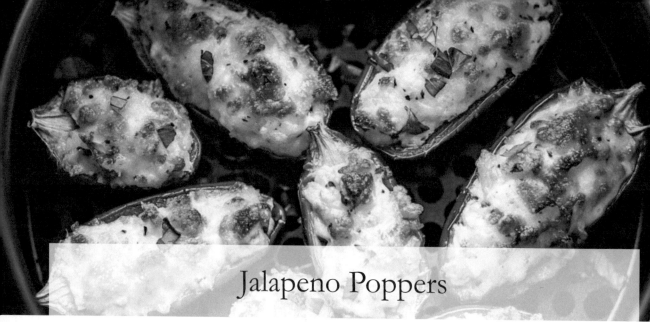

Jalapeno Poppers

 Yield:
4 servings

 Prep Time:
10 minutes

 Cook Time:
10 minutes

 Temperature:
375°F (190°C)

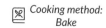 **Cooking method:**
Bake

INGREDIENTS

- 8 jalapeno peppers, halved and seeded
- 4 oz cream cheese, softened
- 1/4 cup shredded cheddar cheese
- 1/4 tsp garlic powder
- Cooking spray

DIRECTIONS

1. Preheat the air fryer to 375°F (190°C).
2. Mix cream cheese, cheddar cheese, and garlic powder. Stuff the jalapeno halves with the mixture.
3. Spray the air fryer basket with cooking spray and place the stuffed jalapenos inside.
4. Bake for 10 minutes or until the tops are golden.
5. Serve warm.

Nutritional Information

140 calories, 3g protein, 4g carbohydrates, 12g fat, 1g fiber, 20mg cholesterol, 180mg sodium, 100mg potassium.

Pita Chips

Yield: 4 servings
Prep Time: 5 minutes
Cook Time: 8 minutes
Temperature: 350°F (175°C)
Cooking method: Roast

INGREDIENTS

- 4 whole wheat pitas, cut into triangles
- 1 tbsp olive oil
- 1/2 tsp garlic powder
- 1/2 tsp paprika
- Salt, to taste

DIRECTIONS

1. Preheat the air fryer to 350°F (175°C).
2. Toss pita triangles with olive oil, garlic powder, paprika, and salt.
3. Place in the air fryer basket and roast for 8 minutes, shaking halfway through.
4. Serve with hummus or dip.

Nutritional Information

110 calories, 3g protein, 14g carbohydrates, 5g fat, 2g fiber, 0mg cholesterol, 150mg sodium, 150mg potassium.

Onion Rings

Yield:
4 servings

Prep Time:
10 minutes

Cook Time:
10 minutes

Temperature:
380°F (195°C)

Cooking method:
Fry

INGREDIENTS

- 1 large onion, sliced into rings
- 1/2 cup breadcrumbs
- 1/4 cup flour

- 1 egg, beaten
- Salt, to taste
- Cooking spray

DIRECTIONS

1. Preheat the air fryer to 380°F (195°C).
2. Coat each onion ring in flour, then dip in beaten egg, and finally coat with breadcrumbs.
3. Spray the air fryer basket with cooking spray and place the onion rings inside.
4. Fry for 10 minutes, flipping halfway through.
5. Serve with dipping sauce.

Nutritional Information

100 calories, 3g protein, 15g carbohydrates, 3g fat, 1g fiber,
20mg cholesterol, 150mg sodium, 100mg potassium.

Cauliflower Tots

Yield: 4 servings   **Prep Time:** 10 minutes   **Cook Time:** 12 minutes   **Temperature:** 375°F (190°C)   **Cooking method:** Fry

INGREDIENTS

- 2 cups grated cauliflower
- 1/4 cup breadcrumbs
- 1/4 cup shredded cheddar cheese
- 1 egg
- 1/4 tsp black pepper

DIRECTIONS

1. Preheat the air fryer to 375°F (190°C).
2. Mix grated cauliflower, breadcrumbs, cheddar cheese, egg, and black pepper in a bowl.
3. Form small tots and place them in the air fryer basket.
4. Cook for 12 minutes or until golden brown, shaking halfway through.
5. Serve with ketchup.

Nutritional Information

90 calories, 5g protein, 9g carbohydrates, 5g fat, 2g fiber, 20mg cholesterol, 150mg sodium, 150mg potassium.

Crispy Tofu Bites

Yield: 4 servings	Prep Time: 5 minutes	Cook Time: 12 minutes	Temperature: 375°F (190°C)	Cooking method: Fry

INGREDIENTS

- 1 block (14 oz) firm tofu, drained and cubed
- 1 tbsp soy sauce (low sodium)
- 1 tbsp cornstarch
- 1/2 tsp garlic powder

DIRECTIONS

1. Preheat the air fryer to 375°F (190°C).
2. Toss tofu cubes in soy sauce, cornstarch, and garlic powder until evenly coated.
3. Place tofu in the air fryer basket and cook for 12 minutes, shaking halfway through.
4. Serve with dipping sauce.

Nutritional Information

120 calories, 10g protein, 5g carbohydrates, 7g fat, 1g fiber, 0mg cholesterol, 250mg sodium, 200mg potassium.

Zucchini Chips

 Yield:
4 servings

 Prep Time:
5 minutes

 Cook Time:
10 minutes

Temperature:
375°F (190°C)

 Cooking method:
Fry

INGREDIENTS

- 2 medium zucchinis, thinly sliced
- 1 tbsp olive oil
- 1/2 tsp salt
- 1/4 tsp black pepper

DIRECTIONS

1. Preheat the air fryer to 375°F (190°C).
2. Toss zucchini slices with olive oil, salt, and pepper.
3. Place in the air fryer basket and fry for 10 minutes, shaking halfway through.
4. Serve immediately.

Nutritional Information

70 calories, 1g protein, 5g carbohydrates, 5g fat, 1g fiber, 0mg cholesterol, 200mg sodium, 200mg potassium.

Spinach & Cheese Stuffed Mushrooms

 Yield:
4 servings

 Prep Time:
10 minutes

 Cook Time:
10 minutes

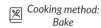 **Temperature:**
350°F (175°C)

Cooking method:
Bake

INGREDIENTS

- 12 large button mushrooms, stems removed
- 1/2 cup fresh spinach, chopped
- 1/4 cup cream cheese, softened
- 1/4 cup grated mozzarella cheese
- 1 garlic clove, minced

DIRECTIONS

1. Preheat the air fryer to 350°F (175°C).
2. In a bowl, mix chopped spinach, cream cheese, mozzarella, and minced garlic. Spoon the mixture into the mushroom caps.
3. Place the stuffed mushrooms in the air fryer basket and bake for 10 minutes or until the cheese is bubbly and mushrooms are tender.
4. Serve warm.

Nutritional Information

80 calories, 3g protein, 4g carbohydrates, 6g fat, 1g fiber, 10mg cholesterol, 150mg sodium, 200mg potassium.

Garlic Parmesan Edamame

 Yield:
4 servings

 Prep Time:
5 minutes

 Cook Time:
8 minutes

Temperature:
390°F (200°C)

 Cooking method:
Roast

INGREDIENTS

- 2 cups frozen shelled edamame, thawed
- 1 tbsp olive oil
- 2 tbsp grated Parmesan cheese
- 1/2 tsp garlic powder
- Salt, to taste

DIRECTIONS

1. Preheat the air fryer to 390°F (200°C).
2. In a bowl, toss the thawed edamame with olive oil, Parmesan cheese, garlic powder, and salt.
3. Place in the air fryer basket and roast for 8 minutes, shaking halfway through.
4. Serve immediately.

Nutritional Information

130 calories, 9g protein, 10g carbohydrates, 7g fat, 3g fiber, 5mg cholesterol, 150mg sodium, 200mg potassium.

Chapter 9: Desserts

Cinnamon Apple Slices

 Yield:
4 servings

 Prep Time:
5 minutes

 Cook Time:
10 minutes

Temperature:
350°F (175°C)

Cooking method:
Bake

INGREDIENTS

- 2 medium apples, cored and sliced
- 1 tbsp melted butter
- 1 tsp ground cinnamon
- 1 tsp honey

DIRECTIONS

1. Preheat the air fryer to 350°F (175°C).
2. Toss apple slices with melted butter, ground cinnamon, and honey.
3. Place the apple slices in the air fryer basket and bake for 10 minutes, shaking halfway through.
4. Serve warm.

Nutritional Information

90 calories, 0g protein, 20g carbohydrates, 3g fat, 3g fiber, 5mg cholesterol, 0mg sodium, 150mg potassium.

Banana Chips

Yield:	Prep Time:	Cook Time:	Temperature:	Cooking method:
4 servings	5 minutes	12 minutes	350°F (175°C)	Roast

INGREDIENTS

- 2 ripe bananas, thinly sliced
- 1 tsp lemon juice
- 1/2 tsp cinnamon

DIRECTIONS

1. Preheat the air fryer to 350°F (175°C).
2. Toss the banana slices with lemon juice and cinnamon.
3. Place the banana slices in the air fryer basket in a single layer and roast for 12 minutes, flipping halfway through.
4. Serve once cooled.

Nutritional Information

60 calories, 1g protein, 16g carbohydrates, 0g fat, 2g fiber, 0mg cholesterol, 0mg sodium, 150mg potassium.

Chocolate-Covered Strawberries

Yield:
4 servings

Prep Time:
5 minutes

Cook Time:
4 minutes

Temperature:
350°F (175°C)

Cooking method:
Fry

INGREDIENTS

- 16 strawberries
- 1/4 cup dark chocolate chips
- 1/2 tsp coconut oil

DIRECTIONS

1. Preheat the air fryer to 350°F (175°C).
2. In a microwave-safe bowl, melt chocolate chips and coconut oil until smooth.
3. Dip each strawberry into the melted chocolate and place on a parchment-lined air fryer basket.
4. Air fry for 4 minutes until the chocolate sets.
5. Serve immediately or refrigerate.

Nutritional Information

80 calories, 1g protein, 10g carbohydrates, 4g fat, 2g fiber, 0mg cholesterol, 0mg sodium, 150mg potassium.

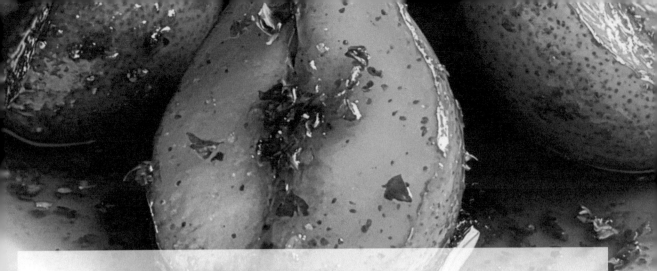

Baked Pears

 Yield:
4 servings

 Prep Time:
5 minutes

 Cook Time:
10 minutes

 Temperature:
350°F (175°C)

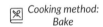 Cooking method:
Bake

INGREDIENTS

- 2 pears, halved and cored
- 1 tbsp maple syrup
- 1/2 tsp ground cinnamon

DIRECTIONS

1. Preheat the air fryer to 350°F (175°C).
2. Drizzle pear halves with maple syrup and sprinkle with cinnamon.
3. Place the pears in the air fryer basket and bake for 10 minutes or until tender.
4. Serve warm.

Nutritional Information

90 calories, 0g protein, 22g carbohydrates, 1g fat, 4g fiber, 0mg cholesterol, 0mg sodium, 170mg potassium.

Mini Blueberry Muffins

 Yield:
6 servings

 Prep Time:
10 minutes

Cook Time:
10 minutes

 Temperature:
325°F (160°C)

Cooking method:
Bake

INGREDIENTS

- 1 cup flour
- 1/4 cup sugar
- 1/2 tsp baking powder

- 1/4 cup unsweetened almond milk
- 1 egg
- 1/2 cup fresh blueberries

DIRECTIONS

1. Preheat the air fryer to 325°F (160°C).
2. In a bowl, mix flour, sugar, baking powder, almond milk, and egg. Gently fold in blueberries.
3. Pour batter into silicone muffin cups and place in the air fryer basket.
4. Bake for 10 minutes or until a toothpick comes out clean.
5. Allow to cool before serving.

Nutritional Information

110 calories, 2g protein, 20g carbohydrates, 3g fat, 1g fiber, 20mg cholesterol, 50mg sodium, 50mg potassium.

Peach Crisp

 Yield:
4 servings

 Prep Time:
5 minutes

 Cook Time:
12 minutes

 Temperature:
350°F (175°C)

 Cooking method:
Bake

INGREDIENTS

- 4 ripe peaches, sliced
- 1/4 cup rolled oats
- 1 tbsp almond flour
- 1 tbsp melted butter
- 1 tsp cinnamon
- 1 tbsp honey

DIRECTIONS

1. Preheat the air fryer to 350°F (175°C).
2. In a bowl, mix oats, almond flour, melted butter, cinnamon, and honey.
3. Place peach slices in the air fryer basket and sprinkle the oat mixture on top.
4. Bake for 12 minutes or until peaches are tender and topping is golden.
5. Serve warm.

Nutritional Information

130 calories, 1g protein, 20g carbohydrates, 5g fat, 2g fiber, 0mg cholesterol, 0mg sodium, 170mg potassium.

Pineapple Rings

 Yield:
4 servings

 Prep Time:
5 minutes

 Cook Time:
8 minutes

Temperature:
375°F (190°C)

 **Cooking method:**
Roast

INGREDIENTS

- 1 fresh pineapple, cut into rings
- 1 tbsp brown sugar
- 1/2 tsp cinnamon

DIRECTIONS

1. Preheat the air fryer to 375°F (190°C).
2. Sprinkle pineapple rings with brown sugar and cinnamon.
3. Place the pineapple rings in the air fryer basket and roast for 8 minutes, flipping halfway through.
4. Serve immediately.

Nutritional Information

70 calories, 0g protein, 18g carbohydrates, 0g fat, 1g fiber, 0mg cholesterol, 0mg sodium, 150mg potassium.

Cinnamon Sugar Donuts

 Yield:
6 servings

 Prep Time:
10 minutes

 Cook Time:
8 minutes

Temperature:
350°F (175°C)

 Cooking method:
Bake

INGREDIENTS

- 1 cup self-rising flour
- 1/4 cup sugar
- 1/4 cup unsweetened almond milk
- 1/4 tsp vanilla extract
- 1 tbsp melted butter
- 1/4 tsp ground cinnamon

DIRECTIONS

1. Preheat the air fryer to 350°F (175°C).
2. Mix flour, sugar, almond milk, and vanilla extract in a bowl to form a dough.
3. Roll out the dough and cut into donut shapes.
4. Place donuts in the air fryer basket and bake for 8 minutes or until golden brown.
5. Brush with melted butter and sprinkle with cinnamon sugar.

Nutritional Information

140 calories, 3g protein, 24g carbohydrates, 4g fat, 1g fiber, 0mg cholesterol, 100mg sodium, 30mg potassium.

Pumpkin Spice Cookies

 Yield:
4 servings

 Prep Time:
10 minutes

 Cook Time:
10 minutes

 Temperature:
325°F (160°C)

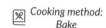 **Cooking method:**
Bake

INGREDIENTS

- 1/2 cup canned pumpkin puree
- 1/4 cup sugar
- 1 cup whole wheat flour
- 1 tsp pumpkin spice
- 1/4 tsp baking soda

DIRECTIONS

1. Preheat the air fryer to 325°F (160°C).
2. In a bowl, mix pumpkin puree, sugar, flour, pumpkin spice, and baking soda until a dough forms.
3. Roll the dough into small balls and place them in the air fryer basket.
4. Bake for 10 minutes or until the cookies are firm.
5. Let cool before serving.

Nutritional Information

90 calories, 2g protein, 18g carbohydrates, 2g fat, 2g fiber, 0mg cholesterol, 30mg sodium, 60mg potassium.

Strawberry Shortcake Bites

 Yield:
4 servings

 Prep Time:
5 minutes

 Cook Time:
8 minutes

Temperature:
350°F (175°C)

 Cooking method:
Bake

INGREDIENTS

- 1 cup diced strawberries
- 1 cup all-purpose flour
- 1/4 cup sugar
- 1/4 cup unsweetened almond milk
- 1/2 tsp vanilla extract

DIRECTIONS

1. Preheat the air fryer to 350°F (175°C).
2. In a bowl, mix flour, sugar, almond milk, and vanilla extract until a dough forms. Gently fold in diced strawberries.
3. Form small balls from the dough and place them in the air fryer basket.
4. Bake for 8 minutes or until golden.
5. Let cool before serving.

Nutritional Information

100 calories, 2g protein, 20g carbohydrates, 2g fat, 1g fiber, 0mg cholesterol, 40mg sodium, 50mg potassium.

CHAPTER 10
30-Day Meal Plan

How to Use the 30-Day Air Fryer Meal Plan: We welcome to your 30-Day Air Fryer Meal Plan!

This guide is designed to help you make the most of your air fryer and bring ease, variety, and delicious flavors to your meals. Using the 30-Day Air Fryer Meal Plan will help you simplify meal preparation, explore diverse flavors, and maintain a balanced, healthy diet. By following the weekly plan, you'll make cooking enjoyable and less stressful—saving time and ensuring that you always have a healthy, delicious meal ready to enjoy. Remember to be flexible, experiment, and most importantly, have fun! Your air fryer is your partner in making everyday cooking easier and more flavorful. Here's a detailed 30-day meal plan using the provided recipes in the Book:

STEP 1 WITH 7-DAY MEAL PLAN

Days	Breakfast	Snack	Lunch	Dinner
Day 1	Avocado Toast with Eggs (Page# 18)	Pita Chips (Page# 75)	Chicken Fajitas (Page# 28)	Garlic Butter Shrimp (Page# 38)
Day 2	Greek Yogurt Pancakes (Page# 14)	Zucchini Chips (Page# 79)	Lemon Garlic Chicken Thighs (Page# 22)	Garlic Butter Shrimp (Page# 38)
Day 3	Tomato and Cheese Breakfast Bake (Page# 20)	Garlic Parmesan Edamame (Page# 81)	Shrimp Tacos (Page# 34)	Lemon Herb Chicken Thighs (Page# 47)
Day 4	Sweet Potato Breakfast Hash (Page# 12)	Crispy Tofu Bites (Page# 65)	Lemon Garlic Chicken Thighs (Page# 22)	Cajun Mahi-Mahi (Page# 44)
Day 5	Breakfast Burritos (Page# 17)	Crispy Tofu Bites (Page# 65)	Roasted Carrots (Page# 29)	Lemon Herb Salmon (Page# 37)
Day 6	Tomato and Cheese Breakfast Bake (Page# 20)	Cauliflower Tots (Page# 77)	Teriyaki Salmon (Page# 24)	Spiced Lamb Chops (Page# 50)
Day 7	Egg and Spinach Breakfast Cups (Page# 13)	Jalapeno Poppers (Page# 74)	Broccoli and Cheese Casserole (Page# 36)	Garlic Lemon Shrimp Skewers (Page# 43)

STEP 2 WITH 8-DAY MEAL PLAN

Days	Breakfast	Snack	Lunch	Dinner
Day 8	Banana Oat Breakfast Bars (Page# 21)	Garlic Parmesan Edamame (Page# 81)	Pesto Chicken Breasts (Page# 32)	Pork Tenderloin with Apples (Page# 41)
Day 9	Breakfast Burritos (Page# 17)	Cauliflower Tots (Page# 77)	Chickpea Salad (Page# 33)	Garlic Lemon Shrimp Skewers (Page# 43)
Day 10	Banana Oat Breakfast Bars (Page# 21)	Pita Chips (Page# 75)	Shrimp Tacos (Page# 34)	Lemon Dill Salmon (Page# 46)
Day 11	Banana Oat Breakfast Bars (Page# 21)	Cauliflower Tots (Page# 77)	Chicken Fajitas (Page# 28)	Crispy Fish Tacos (Page# 45)
Day 12	Greek Yogurt Pancakes (Page# 14)	Mozzarella Sticks (Page# 72)	Pesto Chicken Breasts (Page# 32)	Veggie Stuffed Mushrooms (Page# 40)
Day 13	Greek Yogurt Pancakes (Page# 14)	Onion Rings (Page# 76)	Teriyaki Salmon (Page# 24)	Lemon Herb Salmon (Page# 37)
Day 14	Cinnamon Apple Rings (Page# 19)	Garlic Parmesan Edamame (Page# 81)	Pesto Chicken Breasts (Page# 32)	Lemon Herb Salmon (Page# 37)
Day 15	Breakfast Sausage Patties (Page# 16)	Pita Chips (Page# 75)	Chickpea Salad (Page# 33)	Crispy Fish Tacos (Page# 45)

STEP 3 WITH 8-DAY MEAL PLAN

Days	Breakfast	Snack	Lunch	Dinner
Day 16	Banana Oat Breakfast Bars (Page# 21)	Garlic Parmesan Edamame (Page# 81)	Zucchini Fritters (Page# 23)	Garlic Butter Shrimp (Page# 38)
Day 17	Banana Oat Breakfast Bars (Page# 21)	Garlic Parmesan Edamame (Page# 81)	Broccoli and Cheese Casserole (Page# 36)	Cajun Mahi-Mahi (Page# 44)
Day 18	Berry-Stuffed French Toast (Page# 15)	Cauliflower Tots (Page# 77)	Teriyaki Salmon (Page# 24)	Honey Mustard Chicken Drumsticks (Page# 49)
Day 19	Breakfast Burritos (Page# 17)	Onion Rings (Page# 76)	Turkey Meatballs (Page# 30)	Garlic Butter Shrimp (Page# 38)
Day 20	Greek Yogurt Pancakes (Page# 14)	Mozzarella Sticks (Page# 72)	Chicken Fajitas (Page# 28)	Garlic Lemon Shrimp Skewers (Page# 43)
Day 21	Avocado Toast with Eggs (Page# 18)	Crispy Tofu Bites (Page# 65)	Garlic Parmesan Brussels Sprouts (Page# 26)	Lemon Herb Salmon (Page# 37)
Day 22	Avocado Toast with Eggs (Page# 18)	Spicy Chickpeas (Page# 73)	Roasted Carrots (Page# 29)	Crispy Fish Tacos (Page# 45)
Day 23	Sweet Potato Breakfast Hash (Page# 12)	Pita Chips (Page# 75)	Chicken Fajitas (Page# 28)	Garlic Butter Pork Chops (Page# 48)

STEP 4 WITH 7-DAY MEAL PLAN

Days	Breakfast	Snack	Lunch	Dinner
Day 24	Berry-Stuffed French Toast (Page# 15)	Jalapeno Poppers (Page# 74)	Chicken Fajitas (Page# 28)	Lemon Herb Salmon (Page# 37)
Day 25	Cinnamon Apple Rings (Page# 19)	Cauliflower Tots (Page# 77)	Roasted Carrots (Page# 29)	Garlic Lemon Shrimp Skewers (Page# 43)
Day 26	Cinnamon Apple Rings (Page# 19)	Garlic Parmesan Edamame (Page# 81)	Chicken Fajitas (Page# 28)	Teriyaki Beef Skewers (Page# 52)
Day 27	Cinnamon Apple Rings (Page# 19)	Garlic Parmesan Edamame (Page# 81)	Lemon Garlic Chicken Thighs (Page# 22)	Cajun Mahi-Mahi (Page# 44)
Day 28	Berry-Stuffed French Toast (Page# 15)	Cauliflower Tots (Page# 77)	Garlic Parmesan Brussels Sprouts (Page# 26)	Garlic Butter Pork Chops (Page# 48)
Day 29	Berry-Stuffed French Toast (Page# 15)	Pita Chips (Page# 75)	Chickpea Salad (Page# 33)	Garlic Butter Pork Chops (Page# 48)
Day 30	Cinnamon Apple Rings (Page# 19)	Onion Rings (Page# 76)	Buffalo Cauliflower Bites (Page# 27)	Lemon Herb Salmon (Page# 37)

Conclusion

Conclusion: Mastering the Art of Air Fryer Cooking

Congratulations on reaching the end of **The Ultimate Beginner's Guide to Air Fryer Cooking**! You've taken the first step towards transforming your kitchen routine, exploring the endless possibilities of easy, flavorful, and healthy meals. With every recipe you've tried, you've not only learned to make mouthwatering dishes but also embraced a lifestyle where cooking is simplified, wholesome, and enjoyable.

The air fryer is more than just a kitchen appliance; it's your ticket to effortless cooking that makes every meal an experience worth savoring. From the sizzle of perfectly crisped vegetables to the golden crust on a tender piece of fish, each recipe has been designed to bring out the best flavors using the simplest techniques—all while keeping health at the forefront.

Empowering Your Journey

This cookbook was crafted with you in mind: the busy professional, the loving couple, or the parent striving to make nutritious choices for your family. We understand the challenges of modern life—time constraints, limited ingredients, and the desire to maintain a balanced diet. That's why we provided **dump-and-go recipes**, using pantry staples you already have, so that healthy, tasty meals are always within reach.

You've tackled breakfasts that start your day off right, savory snacks that keep you energized, lunches that nourish your body, and dinners that bring comfort at the end of a long day. The **30-Day Meal Plan** has equipped you with the skills to plan ahead, reduce decision fatigue, and introduce a variety of flavors to your table without the hassle. We hope it has shown you how a little preparation and creativity can transform every meal into something special.

Healthy Eating Made Delicious

One of the primary goals of this cookbook was to show you that healthy food doesn't have to be boring or bland. The air fryer, with its ability to fry, roast, and bake with minimal oil, has proven that you can enjoy crispy, indulgent textures without the guilt.

With each recipe, you've seen how easy it is to create **low-calorie, nutritious dishes** that satisfy your cravings while keeping you on track with your wellness goals.

By incorporating more fresh vegetables, lean proteins, and heart-healthy oils, you've not only nurtured your body but also your mind. Cooking can be therapeutic—a way to unwind, to experiment, and to express love for yourself and those around you.

Your Kitchen, Your Rules

Remember, the goal of this cookbook was to empower you to make cooking approachable, healthy, and most importantly—fun. Life is busy, and mealtime should be a moment of joy, not stress. With these easy, dump-and-go recipes, you now have the confidence to whip up delicious dishes in minutes, all while keeping cleanup simple and your kitchen organized.

The next time you open your pantry, take a look at the ingredients you have, and remember that a delicious meal is just a few steps away. Whether you're craving something crispy, something comforting, or something fresh and light, your air fryer has you covered.

Thank You for Joining the Journey

Thank you for letting this cookbook be a part of your culinary journey. It's been a privilege to guide you through these recipes, and we hope they've brought joy and flavor to your kitchen. Keep experimenting, keep enjoying, and keep cooking with love. The possibilities are endless, and the journey is always delicious.

Now, go on and create your next air fryer masterpiece! 🥂

Kitchen Measurements Conversion Chart

Dry Weights

1/2 OZ	1 tbsp	1/16 C	15 g	-
1 OZ	2 tbsp	1/8 C	28 g	-
2 OZ	4 tbsp	1/4 C	57 g	-
3 OZ	6 tbsp	1/3 C	85 g	-
4 OZ	8 tbsp	1/2 C	115 g	1/4 lb
8 OZ	16 tbsp	1 C	227 g	1/2 lb
12 OZ	24 tbsp	1 1/2 C	340 g	3/4 lb
16 OZ	32 tbsp	2 C	455 g	1 lb

Egg Timer

Soft: 5 min.

Medium: 7 min.

Hard: 9 min.

Oven Temperature

°F	°C	
500	260	10
475	240	9
450	230	8
425	220	7
400	200	6
375	190	5
350	180	4
325	170	3
300	150	2
275	140	1
250	120	1/2
225	110	1/4

Liquid Conversion

1 Gallon
4 quarts
8 pints
16 cups
128 fl oz
3.8 liters

1 Quart
2 pints
4 cups
32 fl oz
946 ml

1 Cup
16 tbsp
8 fl oz
240 ml

1 Pint
2 cups
16 fl oz
470 ml

1/4 Cup
4 tbsp   2 fl oz
12 tsp   60 ml

Liquid Volumes

1 tsp = 5 ml

1 Tbsp = 15 ml

Dash = 1/8 tsp
Pinch = 1/16 tsp

			ml	C	pt	qt
1 OZ	6 tsp	2 tbsp	30 ml	1/8 C	-	-
2 OZ	12 tsp	4 tbsp	60 ml	1/4 C	-	-
2 2/3 OZ	16 tsp	5 tbsp	80 ml	1/3 C	-	-
4 OZ	24 tsp	8 tbsp	120 ml	1/2 C	-	-
5 1/3 OZ	32 tsp	11 tbsp	160 ml	2/3 C	-	-
6 OZ	36 tsp	12 tbsp	177 ml	3/4 C	-	-
8 OZ	48 tsp	16 tbsp	240 ml	1 C	1/2 pt	1/4 qt
16 OZ	96 tsp	32 tbsp	470 ml	2 C	1 pt	1/2 qt
32 OZ	192 tsp	64 tbsp	950 ml	4 C	2 pt	1 qt

Air Fryer Cooking Chart

Vegetables	Temp oF / oC	Time (Min)
Asparagus	400°F/200°C	7
Beet Chips	400°F/200°C	7
Broccoli (Florets)	400°F/200°C	10
Brussels Sprouts (1/2)	380°F/190°C	10
Corn on cob	380°F/190°C	10
Cabbage, Steaks	380°F/190°C	10-12
Carrots, Sliced	400°F/200°C	12
Cauliflower (Florets)	400°F/200°C	10-12
Eggplant, Chunks	400°F/200°C	10-12
Green Beans	400°F/200°C	7-10
Mushrooms	400°F/200°C	8-10
Onions, Chopped	400°F/200°C	10-15
Peppers, Chunks	400°F/200°C	12
Potato, Baby	400°F/200°C	15
Potato, Wedges	400°F/200°C	15
Potato Chips	400°F/200°C	8
Potato, Wedges	400°F/200°C	10
Pumpkin, Chunks	400°F/200°C	12-15
Radish Chips	380°F/190°C	8
Squash	400°F/200°C	12
Squash, Breaded	350°F/170°C	10
Sweet Potato, Fries	400°F/200°C	10
Tomato, Sliced	400°F/200°C	10
Zucchini, Sliced	400°F/200°C	10

Fish and Seafood	Temp oF / oC	Time (Min)
Calamari	400°F/200°C	5
Fish Fillet, 1 inch	400°F/200°C	10-12
Salmon Fillet	400°F/200°C	10-12
Scallops	380°F/190°C	5-7
Shrimp	380°F/190°C	6-8
Shrimp, Breaded	380°F/190°C	8

Meats	Temp oF / oC	Time (Min)
Bacon	380°F/190°C	10
Burgers	380°F/190°C	10
Chicken Whole	350°F/170°C	50-65
Chicken Breast	400°F/200°C	12
Chicken Drumsticks.	400°F/200°C	20-25
Chicken Wings	400°F/200°C	20-25
Chicken Tenders.	400°F/200°C	8
Chicken Thighs	400°F/200°C	20
Filet Mignon	400°F/200°C	8-14
Lamb Chops	400°F/200°C	8-12
Meatballs	400°F/200°C	6-8
Pork Chops	400°F/200°C	12-15
Pork Loin	380°F/190°C	12-18
Ribeye	400°F/200°C	8-12
Ribs	400°F/200°C	10-15
Sausages	400°F/200°C	12-15
Sirloin Steak	400°F/200°C	8-12

Snack/Dessert	Temp oF / oC	Time (Min)
Avocado Fries	380°F/190°C	8
Pineapple, Sliced	350°F/175°C	10-15
Mini Cheesecakes	350°F/175°C	10
Fried Oreos	380°F/190°C	6-8
Fried Pickles	380°F/190°C	8
Jalapenos, Stuffed	380°F/190°C	8-10
Chickpeas	350°F/175°C	15
Blooming Onion	380°F/190°C	10
Pizza	380°F/190°C	8-10
Toast	400°F/200°C	4
Hard Boiled Eggs	350°F/175°C	10-12
Soft Boiled Eggs	350°F/175°C	8-10

Frozen Foods	Temp oF / oC	Time (Min)
Chicken Nuggets	400°F/200°C	8-10
Cheese Sticks	400°F/200°C	7-10
Fish Filets	400°F/200°C	7-10
Frozen Fries	400°F/200°C	14-20
Pot Stickers	400°F/200°C	8-10

INDEX

Made in the USA
Columbia, SC
30 October 2024

45306663R00057